DO YOU ]

- WHY A NORWICH TERRIER OR A LABRADOR RETRIEVER IS A BEST BET FOR KIDS...BUT ROTTWEILERS AND CHOW CHOWS ARE OFF LIMITS?
- WHY PLAYING TUG-OF-WAR WITH YOUR DOG CAN LEAD TO PROBLEMS?
- WHY NEUTERING A MALE DOG IS A MUST?
- HOW TO TEACH YOUR DOG TO ACCEPT, EVEN ENJOY, HAVING HIS TAIL PULLED OR HIS FUR GRABBED?
- HOW TO TELL IF A DOG IS FRIENDLY OR NOT?

# CHILDPROOFING YOUR DOG

AN ESSENTIAL BOOK FOR EVERY FAMILY
WITH A DOG *AND* KIDS

FROM THE ACCLAIMED AUTHOR OF
*GOOD OWNERS, GREAT DOGS*

"Brian Kilcommons, a world-class trainer who has worked for the ASPCA and the Public Broadcasting System's series on veterinary medicine, knows his stuff."

**—*Chicago Sun-Times***

"Brian Kilcommons and Sarah Wilson are knowledgeable, witty guides to the ways and whys of canine behavior."

**—Franklin M. Loew, D.V.M., Ph.D., Dean,
Tufts University School of Veterinary Medicine**

"Trainer Brian Kilcommons shows he doesn't just understand dogs, he understands people and how to get through to them."

**—*Orange County Register***

"Kilcommons is one of the country's most respected dog trainers."

**—*New York* magazine**

# Childproofing Your Dog

## A Complete Guide to Preparing Your Dog for the Children in Your Life

BRIAN KILCOMMONS AND
SARAH WILSON

WARNER BOOKS

A Time Warner Company

*This book is dedicated to Irish, Cookie, Lady,
Tee, Nutmeg, Hannibal, Coco, and Butterfly—the
dogs who began it all and who made our childhoods
rich with wagging tails and friendly faces.*

Warner Books, Inc., 1271 Avenue of the Americas, New York, NY 10020
A Time Warner Company
Visit our Web site at http://warnerbooks.com

Printed in the United States of America
First Printing: April 1994
10 9 8

LIBRARY OF CONGRESS CATALOGING-IN-PUBLICATION DATA
Kilcommons, Brian.
Childproofing your dog: a complete guide to preparing your dog
for the children in your life/Brian Kilcommons and Sarah Wilson.
p.   cm.
Includes bibliographical references and index.
ISBN 0-446-67016-2
1. Dogs—Training. 2. Dogs—Social aspects. 3. Children and ani-
mals.   I. Wilson, Sarah, 1960- .   II. Title.
SF431.K53   1994
636.7´0887—dc20          93-37837
CIP

*Cover design by Julia Kushnirsky
Cover photograph by Sarah Wilson
Book design by Kathryn Parise*

# Contents

# Introduction

From personal experience, we both know the richness and wonder animals add to childhood. Scientists of all types are now studying the positive effects pets have on children. They discuss the development and enrichment of bonding, responsibility, stability, and empathy. Anyone raised with a dog can confirm this. The waking up in the middle of the night frightened by a dream and hugging the pet close. The ridiculous games played with the tolerant dog. The happily wagging tail saying all is well to a child coming home to an empty house. The uncritical friend, lying quietly next to the bed of a youngster recovering from some childhood crisis. The curious companion tagging along on a walk through the woods.

This book is written in the hopes of passing on this magic. In order to get the most out of *Childproofing Your Dog,* you must first build a foundation of communication and understanding between you and your dog through command training. This is a project in and of itself, so we have supplied a bibliography to help you find the information you need to do this successfully. We supply basic information when needed, but to fully understand how a dog thinks and learns, please read one of the recommended books. And if you haven't already undertaken basic command training, don't delay any longer. The techniques described in *Childproofing* will work to best advantage—and your child's safety is best served—when such training is in place.

To childproof something means to take measures to make it as safe as possible for your child. But with all the changes you may make in your home, for example, there is no guarantee that your child won't bump his head on the bookshelf or scrape her knee in the driveway. Childproofing is about preventing the preventable as much as that is humanly possible. That's exactly what this book is about. It is no promise that your dog, or any other dog, will never harm a child. But it does give you many steps and exercises that you can do with your dog and your child to help them avoid some of the most common problems.

Our childhood memories of our pets are endless. And all the while, our wonderful canine companions were teaching us about responsibility, thoughtfulness, loyalty, consistency of the heart, and what it is to love—without either of us even knowing what we were learning. Neither of us would ever voluntarily be without a dog in our lives. Neither of us can even imagine it. Dogs are too interwoven in our vision of the world. We created this book so that more people can enjoy the gifts that dogs have to offer without the worries or concerns that misunderstanding and miscommunication can bring.

—*Brian Kilcommons and Sarah Wilson*

# 1

# The Family Dog

*"Choose a dog as carefully as you would
a housemate."*

Ajax, a young Weimaraner, dragged eight-year-old Ellen into our office, in the process yanking the lead out of Ellen's hand. Mr. and Mrs. Woods came in after. "How did you choose Ajax?" I began.

"The man at the pet store recommended this breed for the city. We've never had a dog before. We wanted a calm, easy one. He said Weimaraners weren't too active and would be good with our little girl."

I shook my head in disagreement. "No, Weimaraners are as active as they come and strong willed as well." Ajax would have been a fine choice for an active, experienced dog owner but not for an inexperienced, basically sedentary, urban family.

This first chapter addresses the questions you should consider when choosing your family dog: Do you really want a dog? How old should the children be when you get a puppy? Is a male or female better for a family? Which breeds make the best family dogs? Where do you get a good dog, and how do you select a puppy or adult dog? We begin with what makes a good family dog.

## A good family dog...

### ...fits in with your lifestyle

If you jog daily, by all means get an active dog but don't think that you will become a triathlete when you get a dog. It won't happen. Assume things will stay the same and choose accordingly.

### ...tolerates touch or noise and forgives mistakes

Some dogs are more physically sensitive than others. Hunting breeds had to run through briars and tolerate the sound of guns to do their job. Some of the tiny breeds, however, bred solely to cuddle, hate rough handling. To work well in the average family, dogs must accept noise, lots of touching and be forgiving.

### ... calms himself once excited

The ability to calm down—to stop barking once the guest is inside, to relax after the child has stopped pulling his tail—is critical to being an easy and safe family companion.

### ... likes people

Pet-store puppies who have been in cages for too long or kennel-raised older dogs may never have much interest in you or your children. Shy dogs may eventually accept the immediate family but often don't adjust to your child's playmates. Look for a pup that has been handled every day, was raised in the house, preferably around well-behaved, well-supervised children.

# *Q and A*

### *Do you really want a dog?*

A dog is work, no two ways around it. And if you have room in your life for one more responsibility, then consider a canine companion. If you're getting it for the kids, or because your partner wants it, or because you think a family ought to have a dog, think again. This is not a decoration but a living, breathing individual who will need daily walks, interaction, care, training, guidance, and supervision, especially during puppyhood. Our clients constantly tell us "I had no idea this was so much work." It is. Pleasant if you have the time, energy, and desire; irritating if you thought you were buying Lassie, who would grace your life with few demands. The benefits of dog ownership are immense, adding stability, acceptance, joy, and security when all these things seem hard to come by, but these benefits are not without demands on your time, income, and energy.

### *How old should my kids be when I get a dog?*

The best time to get a dog is after your child is age four, maybe even five if you want to raise a puppy. Younger children do not have the mental understanding or physical ability to be consistently gentle. If you have younger children and a dog, read the relevant sections and SUPERVISE! People sometimes want to get a new puppy when the child is an infant on the theory that they'll grow up together. Save yourself the stress and exhaustion—one baby at a time please!

### *Which breed is best?*

Man created each breed to perform a specific task. These tasks still influence your dog's behavior today. Your Labrador may never retrieve a duck, but this will not stop him from wanting to retrieve everything that is not nailed down. Your Jack Russell may never kill a rat, but he is probably still the feisty "you start it and I'll finish it" kind of guy that could get the job done.

Read about the breed you are interested in and think about how that heritage might still affect your pet's behavior today. In general, dogs bred to work closely with man and for low levels of aggression are better family dogs than those dogs developed for their fighting, killing, or aggressive prowess.

A classic example of a breed created to work closely with man while not being too aggressive is the Golden Retriever. Their wonderful temperament has won them millions of fans through the years. Unfortunately, today, it is possible to find shy, hyperactive, and aggressive Goldens. When a breed is popular, be careful where you get your pet.

Mixed-breed dogs are every ounce as good as the most blue-blooded purebred dog. The only difference for our purposes is predictability. When you buy a Labrador, you know, generally, how big he'll be and how much coat he'll have. Mixed breeds are a kaleidoscope of their special combination, history, and environment. If you don't mind a bit of mystery in your life, get a mixed-breed pup. He'll greet you at the door, bark at the stranger on your porch, and fetch a ball for your kids just as well as any purebred.

### *Puppy or adult dog?*

Puppies are cute, demanding, and unfettered by any understanding of human rules. You need the time, energy, and patience to teach them everything from "Don't run through the house with my underwear in your mouth" to "Don't rip off the wallpaper." Puppies are usually not the best choice for a household with children under the age of five.

Adult dogs are often housebroken and past the intense chewing stage. On the down side, bad habits are sometimes firmly in place. Old dogs can learn new tricks, though, so don't rule them out. The older dog is a fine choice for many families. In our experience, they bond to their new family just as well, and in some cases better, than puppies.

### *Male or female?*

We've owned and loved both. Regardless of sex, family pets should be neutered. Neutered dogs—both male and female—are calmer, less aggressive, and less prone to hormonal mood swings. Neutering at a young age helps prevent certain negative behaviors like leg lifting or dominance aggression from developing. Neutered pets live longer, healthier lives, so don't wait. The bottom line about gender is that dogs are individuals, and while generalities about males and females can be made, we don't find them all that useful. The only generality worth noting is that unneutered male dogs bite people the most. *Neuter your dog.*

### *Where should I get my dog?*

The best sources for a good pet are reputable breeders, word of mouth, rescue groups, and animal shelters.

## Reputable Breeders

A good breeder breeds only two or three litters a year, asks you lots of questions, and tells you about the breed—good and bad. A bad breeder sells you a puppy with few questions asked. A bad breeder always seems to have puppies, often breeding four or more litters a year. Don't be fooled by "AKC Registered." AKC papers are like a car title—a Rolls Royce has a title and so does the rusted-out junk car that won't start.

Good breeders know their dogs. You'll be able to meet at least one of the pup's parents and should like the parent. The apple does not usually fall far from the tree with dogs, and if your potential pup's mother is too protective, nervous, or whatever for you to meet and handle, skip her pups. You want a friendly, outgoing, stable pet, and those come most often from friendly, stable, outgoing parents. Home-raised pups, especially those raised with well-behaved and supervised children, are your best bet.

## Word of Mouth

People move, schedules change, and good dogs need new homes. Tell local veterinarians, groomers, trainers, and pet-supply stores (that don't sell dogs) what you are looking for and then be willing to wait. There is an old saying in the dog world: "The right time to get a dog is when the right dog comes along." Resist the temptation to rush. A good dog is worth some patience and research.

### Pure-Breed Rescue Groups

Almost every breed club has a handful of dedicated people who locate, rescue, care for, and then adopt out individual dogs of their chosen breed. We have used these groups for both locating and placing animals and have been very happy with the results. Call the AKC, 1-919-233-9767, to get the number of the national club for the breed you are interested in. Contact the club and ask them who does their rescue work.

### Animal Shelters

Every area has a shelter that houses lost, abandoned, and stray dogs. These hardworking places can be wonderful sources. Many animals end up there because their owners were less than ideal, not because the dogs were. Talk to the kennel people, ask them what dogs might work for you. Go back a few times. If you are serious, a shelter is usually happy to help. Remember: The dog that fits in with your family is a beautiful dog. Don't let superficial beauty be the deciding factor. Too many people go hunting for a certain "look," not realizing that looks do not a companion make. Seek out a wonderful, calm, happy dog, and then learn to love what it looks like.

## *Selecting a Puppy*

If you want a calm, relaxed adult dog, choose a calm, relaxed pup. Choose for stability, ability to calm itself, forgiveness, touch sensitivity, noise tolerance, and attachment to people. This is easy to do if you know a few simple tests.

### Stability

Is the pup leaping at your face, nipping your nose, yanking on your shoelaces? Skip over him, that kind of energy can be hard to live with. Skip any that cower in the corner, too. Instead, choose the pup who comes right up to you, doesn't mouth much, and isn't frantic.

### Ability to Calm Down

Cradle a pup upside down in your arms like a baby. Does he struggle? Does he mouth? Struggling that increases and mouthing that becomes frantic are signs that he can't calm himself down. Skip him. Also skip the puppy who lies stiff in your arms. This frightened pup may not react well to a child's normal play. Instead, select the pup who lies in your arms relaxed and happy. A little mouthing and struggling is normal, but he should settle down.

### Touch Sensitivity and Forgiveness

Pick up a puppy and take hold of the skin between his toes. Apply pressure until you get a response. Does he bite at your hand? Does he scream like he's being

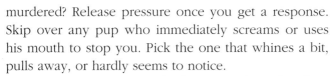

murdered? Release pressure once you get a response. Skip over any pup who immediately screams or uses his mouth to stop you. Pick the one that whines a bit, pulls away, or hardly seems to notice.

Forgiveness is measured after you release his foot. Does he immediately relax and maybe start licking you? That's the right response. If he seems distrustful or withdrawn, skip him. An unforgiving pup is almost always trouble. Things will happen to your pet, especially with children around, so forgiveness is critical.

## Noise Tolerance

Noise tolerance is important if you have children. Dogs who are frightened of noises make every toddler-related crash and every noise-making toy an event. Drop a set of keys near the pups. Some pups will startle and then investigate. Others won't even notice. These are good choices for noisy households. Skip the pups who run for cover and stay there.

## Attachment to People

Sit with all the pups for ten minutes or so. Look for the pup who stays near you. Any pup who does not come over to say hello within a minute should be avoided. If one pup is constantly nipping you, skip him as well. Every puppy has an individual personality. Each litter contains a range of personalities. Chances are you'll find a couple of pups who are friendly, stable, and attracted to people. Select your new pet from one of these.

## Selecting an Adult Dog

When you look at an older dog, do not judge him on how he behaves with you; after all, he doesn't know you. Watch how he is with "his" people, if you can. If he's friendly and calm with them, that's a good sign. If he is uncontrollable, stay clear. Look for one who lives with children and likes them. Beware of dogs who have spent their lives tied up. Chances are they aren't really housebroken and lack social graces. Don't pass over a three- to four-year-old dog; they can slide into your home as if they had been there forever.

When selecting an adult dog from a shelter, speak to the staff. Often they know the nice dogs and can give you an inside lead on one. Next, take a walk through the kennels. This is always noisy. If you are bringing your child(ren) with you, it may be worth bringing earplugs. Your kids will be more comfortable and can focus on looking at the dogs. No hands or fingers in cages!

When you walk up and down the aisles, keep an ear open. Many dogs will bark when you are right in front of the cage, but beware the one that keeps on yapping long after you're past. It may be a sign he's having a hard time calming himself down and could be noisy to live with. The dog you want may bark his hello, but, when you move on, he settles down.

The ideal dog was raised with kids, comes up to the front of the cage eagerly, and quiets down pretty quickly once you're past. There will probably be two or three like this on any one visit. Next, let your kid(s) walk toward the cages. Have them speak calmly and in a friendly manner. Remember, keep hands and fingers outside! Does the dog seem interested in the child? Is he friendly? That's great! Backing away or refusing to say hello are not good signs.

You probably have a couple of animals in mind now. Ask the staff if they may be taken out of the cages one at a time. Most dogs are pretty wild when they first come out of confinement. That's to be expected and often does not reflect the dog's true nature. Talk to him softly; scratch under his neck and chin. If he calms down a bit, it's a good sign, but don't expect him to act as if he knows you—he doesn't.

Once you find a dog that is friendly to the kids, not too barky, and calms down a bit when given a chance, adopt her. If it makes things easier, ask the shelter to hold her for a few hours while you go out and buy her crate, food (the same brand she's been eating, please), toys, bowls, brushes, and other necessities of dog-owning life. That way you'll be all set up when you bring her home. Don't be surprised if she's a bit depressed the first few days. No matter where you get your adult dog, a new home is a big change. Give her some time. Go to your vet as soon as possible to make sure she does not have parasites, ear infections, or other problems. If she hasn't been neutered, do so immediately.

Start obedience work right away using fun, positive methods. Structure and routine is the best medicine for a newly adopted dog. Not only will it build the bond between you, but it reassures her that all is well and that a knowledgeable leader is at the helm.

Then enjoy her, but we don't have to tell you that, do we?

# 2

# *Before Baby*

*"The more changes you make before the baby arrives
the fewer problems you'll have afterwards."*

Tessa, an exuberant Golden Retriever, is just too bright to be easy to live with. Pushy and adorable, she is doted on by her owners, soon-to-be parents. Although they worry about her habit of eating strange things, like rocks and disposable razors, they "do not have the heart" to control her. Tessa is a mess. I warned them: "Decide now what behaviors you want and don't want, or you'll have problems later." They have problems.

An attention addict, Tessa continues to leap at them for petting, only now they have an infant in their arms. The cute grabbing of clothing she has always done is now dangerous when she grabs the baby blanket. When given half a chance, the dog runs to the crib and starts barking.

Before your baby arrives, think about how your life will change. Imagine your dog's behavior around an infant. If you see potential problems, address them now. Behaviors do not go away on their own, but you can change them with some commonsense planning.

## *Changes to Make before the Baby Arrives*

### Plan Your Schedule

Dogs thrive on routine. Establish a reasonable schedule for your dog before the baby arrives, and then stick to it. This includes walking times, play periods, mealtimes, and anything else you can think of. You may want, for example, to move your dog's long exercise walk and play period from early in the morning, when you're bound to be tired, to the late afternoon.

Exercise is the best problem preventative there is. Before your due date, arrange for a friend to help with the dog after the baby's arrival. If you are fortunate enough to live next to a jogger, see if the dog can go along. Maybe the teenager next door would like a few extra dollars for running your dog. Almost every neighborhood has such resources if you start asking around early.

You may never need the help. You may give birth easily with no complications to a child who sleeps eight hours a night from the day you bring him or her home. You could also win the lottery. If you don't, the last thing you'll need or want to be doing for the first few months is running the dog around at 6:00 A.M., twenty minutes after Junior has finally fallen asleep.

All the planning is great for the dog, but we are really recommending it for your comfort. A dog who is on a routine and is well exercised is less likely to be competitive, anxious, or demanding of your attention. In today's world, where so few stresses can be controlled, regulating this one can give you a needed break.

## Make the Dog Work for a Living

A dog who gets a free ride often develops a poor atti-tude. After all, her bills are paid, her needs attended to, and adult human beings fawn over her, all day long, for no apparent reason. This kind of treatment makes a dog think that you live to serve her. Start making the dog pull her own weight. When your dog wants atten-tion, make her sit first. (Say the command once; then gently guide her into position with one hand on her collar and one hand on her rear.) Tell her how sweet she is, and let it go at that. Ignore her completely until the next command. This teaches her that good things come from listening to you. Think of it as the doggy version of please and thank you.

## Change Furniture Rights

Soon your baby is going to be napping on the couch or lying on the bed. To avoid any mishaps, teach your dog to stay on the floor unless invited up with a clear com-mand like "Up!" Should your enthusiastic furniture jumper leap up uninvited, dismiss him with an "Off." If he is resistant, leave a lead and collar on him. When he jumps up, command "Off," and guide him off with short little snaps of the lead. Once on the floor, praise him for being so brilliant! When it is OK for him to come up, make him sit on command, and then invite him up with a pat on the couch and a clear "OK, up!" When he obeys, praise him warmly. He'll soon start politely waiting for your invitation before making himself comfortable.

## Watch Your Mouth!

Your dog takes you literally. For his whole life, your dog has heard "What a good little boy" thrown at him in the kindest possible way. For his whole life, he has come up for an ear scratch and a pat when those words are spoken. You have taught him that those words are for him and him alone.

Now your child arrives. You lean over the newborn face and coo, "How's Mommy's good little boy?" All of a sudden you have a furry face shoved between you and your infant. Soft brown eyes say, "Here I am! Want to pet me?" You push him away and say, "Don't be jealous!" He's not "jealous," he's confused. He's simply responding to the words he's been trained to think of as his.

Avoid this confusion by developing some new key phrases for your dog and only your dog. "What a good dog!" is a universally acceptable one that, we hope, you are unlikely to use with your infant. If you choose a few phrases and stick to them, your dog will soon learn that these are your terms of love. Make this change as soon as possible!

## Stop Wild Games in the House

A dog in pursuit of a ball will jump over, or onto just about anything. With an infant or a toddler around, fetch games are best relegated to outdoors, away from the child. An unpredictable bounce of a ball can lead to an unanticipated pounce of a puppy.

It is a good plan to keep a leash on your dog for the first few weeks after your baby comes home. Now you'll be able to stop any unwanted behavior as it begins.

## Ignore the Dog

When you are expecting, all the parental juices are flowing. The likely recipient of these urges is the family dog. The temptation, before the baby arrives, is to give your pet extra attention, since pretty soon you won't have as much time. This good intention paves the way for future problems. Extra attention will lead the dog to expect it. Dogs, like the rest of us, get used to luxuries easily. When that attention is suddenly shifted to the child, it is both unfair to the dog and sets the stage for competition between the dog (prince) and the infant (intruder).

Do everyone a favor and dethrone your dog before the baby ever enters the picture. A good rule to follow is no more than ten minutes of attention per hour when you are home. If that seems harsh, then you already have a problem!

We want your baby's arrival to be a welcome event, not the beginning of trouble. If your dog takes to the new addition well, then you can safely increase the attention he's getting, but until then, limit it. This way, when the baby arrives and your attention is elsewhere, there will be no radical change in your dog's life.

In fact, if you link the baby's presence with a little extra attention, your dog will soon look forward to the tyke being around. An easy way to do this is to speak kindly to the dog as you go into the child's room. Include him in what you are doing, be extra warm to him when he is around the child, and the rest of the time pretty much ignore him. Soon he'll be wagging his tail whenever you approach the baby.

## Expose Your Dog to Children

Unless exposed to children, many dogs will not know how to react to them. The best possible thing you can do is have well-behaved and well-supervised children around your puppy. But whether you have a pup or an adult dog, the rules are the same.

Invite friends who have children to visit, or visit them. Keep your dog on lead. It's important that you have complete control during the first few meetings. Stay relaxed. If you are nervous, your dog is likely to blame the children and become distrustful of the young ones.

Have the children ignore the dog initially. Walk the dog over and have the children give her a treat. Praise her happily and let her sniff if she wants to. Children have a different scent than adults, and the dog will need to get used to it. Make sure the kids stay calm; no running, shouting, or jumping around. If at any time you feel the least discomfort about your dog's reaction to children, seek professional assistance.

Next, take the dog around more-active children. Take a walk on lead around town or in a local park, and do some obedience work. This reassures her that you are in charge and that all is well. Secondly, sound happy. Your dog takes her cues from you, and if you're happy, she's more likely to have fun.

Some dogs may bark when the children yell or run. If this happens, do not soothe your dog. She will misinterpret that as praise and bark more! Stay calm, do obedience work, and keep some distance away from the kids. Over time, she'll get used to their ways. If you feel unsure about your dog's reaction, get professional help. This is not something to try to rectify by yourself!

*18*

# FOOLISH PREPARATIONS

The story in the English newspaper told of a young mother who stepped out to the corner store, leaving her newborn napping and the dog loose in the apartment. She returned to find that her infant had been mauled by her pet. This seemed a strange scenario, so I read on.

The story told of how the mother had "prepared" the dog for the baby by getting a life-size baby doll for the dog to play with. Apparently the father had played Tug-of-War with the dog using the baby doll. Unwittingly, these parents had trained their dog to treat the baby as a plaything. If only they'd known that everything we do instructs our dogs, they would have realized they were teaching their dog to play Tug-of-War with their infant!

### POINTS TO PONDER

- Do not promote aggressive or competitive games with your dog. Such games may unwittingly teach your pet to play aggressively. Avoid trouble; play the games outlined on pages 60 to 63.
- Never, but never, leave a dog alone with a small child—for the safety of both. Neither one is capable of knowing what they should and should not be doing.
- If the dog had been crated (see page 27) or otherwise confined away from the child, none of this could have happened.

## Train Your Dog to Leave the Baby's Toys Alone

By purchasing baby toys ahead of time and teaching your dog to leave them alone, you can save yourself a lot of irritation. It is easier to teach this when the toys are new and therefore relatively uninteresting. After baby has spit up on, smeared food into, and dragged the toys around for a bit, they become considerably more fascinating to a dog.

### Which One Is Yours?

Before you begin, make it easy on your dog by choosing toys for your baby that are different from those you have for your dog. If the dog loves latex toys, skip them for your baby. Don't give your dog a stuffed animal to play with, and then wonder why he's running off with your child's teddy bear.

Start off easy. Put down an unappealing baby toy, and holding on to your dog, toss his favorite toy over by it. Release your dog while you say in an excited tone "Which one is yours?" Encourage him to go over and get his. If he picks up the baby's, calmly tell him "Leave it," and take the toy out of his mouth. Then excitedly go to his, wave it enticingly in front of him, and tell him "This one's yours! That's a good dog! Get this one!" Let him take it. Repeat this until he consistently gets his and only his. As he comes to understand this game, add in more and different toys. Keep note of which baby toys he has a hard time ignoring, and move on to the scent-marking technique.

## Scent-Marking Baby's Toys

If the dog's having trouble getting the hang of the Which One Is Yours? game, try scent-marking your child's toys. Put a dab of Listerine on each of the baby's toys. Use a tiny dab; if you can barely smell it, that's perfect. Your dog's sense of smell is far better than ours, he'll be able to tell. Then play Which One Is Yours? with him. Mark the toys once a week for a month; then simply mark every new toy that is given to the child. He will soon catch on.

## Booby-Trapping

Now that he understands the game and plays it pretty well, you can begin booby-trapping the baby toys, especially the ones he has a hard time passing up. Make up a few shake cans: rinse out empty soda cans, put fifteen pennies in each and tape them shut. Put them on a shelf or table. Put a baby toy below. Tie thread to the toy, run the thread up to the cans and tape it to them. When your dog takes the toy, the cans will tumble down after him. Very effective for most dogs. Only set these up when you are home to supervise. Otherwise some dogs may recover from the surprise and chew the toy.

# Q and A

*Our dog's like a child to us. Do we have to make all these changes?*

From what our clients have told us, parenthood often takes them by surprise. Having an infant overwhelmed them in the best possible way. Many of them never knew that such strong love was possible. It's not that you don't love your pet; it's just that for a while it is eclipsed by the total involvement with the child.

Of course, you may stay calm, cool, and balanced, but don't bet your life savings on it. By anticipating any changes, you can take real steps to making the transition smooth and easy for your dog. Preparation is seldom wasted. If it turns out that nothing has changed, going back to the way it was will be easy. But if things do change, then your pet will be well prepared. Deny it, prolong it, or ignore it, and you invite problems.

*My dog is frightened of children. Why is that?*

There are many reasons that a dog may be frightened of children, but the most common one is that he just doesn't know what they are. If he has never been exposed to kids, he may react to them as you might to seeing little green men on the street. Read the section in this chapter on exposing your dog to children. Usually after a few good experiences, most dogs accept children into their concept of the human race. But if you have one of the few dogs that just doesn't accept children easily, get some help. Usually this can be worked out with patience and perseverance.

### *My dog growls at children. What can I do?*

Duchess, a two-year-old West Highland White Terrier, lay asleep by her masters' feet as the expectant parents told me their concerns. "We're having a baby in April," they said, "and Duchess growls at children."

"When did this start?" I asked.

"That's what's so peculiar about it," they replied, puzzled. "She used to be so good with children. The first time my nephew met her, she loved him. He could do anything to her—pick her up, hold her. He even kicked her, and she just wagged her tail. But the next time, she started this growling business."

Dogs don't like to be hurt. If children hurt them, they will not like children. Protect your dog from harm, and control the children your dog comes in contact with. If the child refuses to be gentle, remove your dog or remove the child. Do not allow your dog to be hurt. If your dog is inadvertently injured by a child, be sure to counter that experience by visiting with calm, well-mannered children who will give him treats and pet him gently.

But if he is hurt and decides a strong offense is the best defense, get help. Aggression is not a fix-at-home problem. Dogs do not grow out of aggression; they grow into it. If your dog growls at a child, get the help of a qualified trainer immediately.

The good news is that most dogs are good with good kids. If your dog is normally good with kids but seems to dislike or be frightened of a particular child, take your dog's word for it. He probably has a good reason. Keep him with you when that child is around so you can supervise what's going on.

# 3

# *Bringing Home Baby*

*"Hope for the best, prepare for the worst."*

Jean felt terrible for her Shetland Sheepdog, Donner. He was being displaced by the baby. She did not want her dear little friend to feel badly, so she showered him with extra love and attention. Whenever the dog startled at the baby's movements or sounds, Jean quickly picked him up and soothed him. By the time I arrived, Donner was a shivering bundle of nerves who cowered and snarled whenever the baby moved or squealed. Jean did not mean to train her dog to be afraid, but that's exactly what she did by petting and praising him every time he was frightened. This chapter is all about teaching your dog to be relaxed, undemanding, and sensible around a baby.

Bringing home a new infant is an exciting moment overshadowed in too many households with a nervous question like "I wonder how the dog will react?" Visions of some kind of disaster fill the minds of new parents. These fears are usually unfounded. This is a time of expanding family and contracting free time. This is not the time to have to worry, dote, befriend, or coo over your dog.

## Bringing Home Baby: The First Meeting

For everything to go as smoothly as possible, have someone give your dog a good run before you all arrive. A quick obedience session is a good idea, too. When you arrive, one of you stay with the baby while the other greets the dog. This gives you a chance to say hello without worry, and an opportunity to get control. Don't allow jumping or hysteria. Insist that she sit and stay seated while you pet her and say hello. If this is difficult, put her lead on and step on it at the point where it touches the ground when she's standing. Now if she jumps, she'll correct herself! Ignore her antics until she settles down a bit. Touch and speak to her calmly. Not only will this calm her down, but she'll have a chance to get the baby's scent from your hands and clothing. Keep your praise warm and relaxed. If you want the dog to be calm, you stay calm.

Now bring in the baby. Have one adult carry the infant while another handles the dog, who is, of course, on lead. Stay calm. Do not focus on the dog meeting the baby, that will happen soon enough. Just go about your business and bring the dog along on lead. She may not even notice the child, and that is fine. If she jumps, tell her "Off," correct her with a quick sideways snap of the lead if necessary, and then have her sit.

When she notices the baby, she'll most likely come over for a thorough sniff, perhaps a lick, and then get on to more interesting things. Quietly praise the dog during this. The greeting now over, life goes on. Allow the dog to drag her lead behind as she trots about her business. Keep to your routine, and chances are your dog will readily adjust.

## ODE TO A CRATE

Dogs, like people, need privacy. If your dog has been a nine-to-five dog and suddenly you're home and the baby's home and friends and family are around, it just may be more than he can handle. Having a crate and a crating schedule, gives him routine rest periods. Something we all can use!

Crates are also safety equipment. Like a car seat or a bicycle helmet, they are just a sensible precaution. Dogs and young children should not be left alone together. Even the world's most tolerant dog may become unnerved if a child sticks a pencil in his ear. Kids are kids, dogs are dogs, and that's why there are crates.

Also, you'll need quiet time for yourself. The baby can get cranky and you can get tired or just overwhelmed. (Let's not even talk about the hormonal backflips that may be going on.) With all the demands on you, you need a place to put the dog when you just can't handle one more thing! Putting your dog in the crate for a few hours won't cause him any harm and will do everyone a lot of good. No guilt necessary—just accept yourself and cope accordingly.

You'll get in trouble only if you start trying to be all things to all people and dogs. Personally, we would not raise a dog without one!

## *Teaching Your Dog to Accept Childlike Handling*

Adults are boring. We tend to pet our dogs the same way all the time, speaking in the same moderate tones. Only when we want to play with the dog do we speak more excitedly. Not only do we sound more excited, but we tend to move more erratically, often kneeling on the floor while we do it. Now we have set the stage for problems.

Enter a baby. Babies grab, hold, tug, pull, poke, and yank. They squeal. They gurgle. Their movement is jerky. They crawl on the floor. What's a dog to think? Is the child playing? Even though your baby may not be moving around a lot yet, he will be soon. It's our job to teach the dog what to expect before a child gets mobile.

As with all of this type of training, please do it out of sight of any older children. Children are great imitators. We don't need them doing these things to the dog. Quite the opposite; they should be encouraged to be careful and gentle with dogs at all times. But if they forget, or if one of their friends does not know, these exercises will teach your dog to accept it all in good humor.

## How Does That Grab You?

As you pet your dog, gently grab a hunk of skin and wiggle it. Praise him; then release and praise some more. Wasn't that fun? When he accepts this happily, start grabbing more quickly and more firmly. Never harshly! This is not supposed to be painful. What a good dog! Give him a treat! Soon your dog will associate this type of grabbing with fun and wag his tail accordingly.

## How about a Hug?

Children love to hug dogs. They should be taught not to, but just in case, prepare your dog. While you are praising the dog, give a quick, gentle hug; then release. Praise! Over a few days, as the dog comes to accept this type of handling, slowly hold for longer periods. Always release before the dog gets frightened or uncomfortable. Work up to a twenty- to thirty-second hug, always followed by lots of praise. Don't rush him. The idea is to make this fun. If he pulls away, then for three days give him attention ONLY when you are hugging him. That should change his mind. If at any time he growls or lifts a lip, stop and contact a qualified trainer or behaviorist near you.

## Screams and Squeals

Children squeal, bellow, yell, bray, and giggle with glee. Dogs can be confused by this. It's pretty common for a dog to associate loud voices with trouble. If a dog's been hurt or frightened by a human, it's usually been with a loud voice in his ears. Later, when he hears children being children, he may become tense. To solve this problem, begin, in the privacy of your own home, to get the dog used to various tones and volumes of voice. First and foremost, stop any hitting of or yelling at the dog! There are better ways to teach your dog than that. Hitting teaches the dog to fear fast movements, and children specialize in fast movements! Yelling creates a fear of loud voices, and again, loud sounds are a sine qua non of childhood.

Begin by getting your companion used to sudden sound bursts by walking toward him, loudly saying "Dog!" and then praising him quietly and warmly. As he adjusts, work up to running up to him while yelling "DOG!" Make it a game that always ends with warm praise and petting. Do not use an angry voice. Practice instead with a variety of volume and tone. Make it a game, have fun. If the dog is spooked, move more slowly, speak more softly and praise more enthusiastically. Make some recordings of children making noise, and play it daily when he is eating. This way he'll associate something pleasant (eating) with the sound of children. He will soon adjust.

## ROOM SERVICE PLEASE!

The little spaniel, Pretty, sniffed me briefly before retreating to her corner. "Ever since we had the baby, she just lies there. We spend lots of time with her in her corner, petting her and telling her that we still love her," said the father. "She'll only eat from our hands. Is she going to be all right?"

"I think so," I answered. "She's just enjoying the room service."

Pretty, initially surprised by the new addition, chose a safe spot to watch the new goings-on. The owners interpreted this as depression and set about giving her all kinds of attention when she was in that corner. Pretty quickly surmised that the best way to get love was to lie there. Inadvertently, by praising, attention, and food, they had trained Pretty to lie in the corner. Solution? Ignore her when she's in her corner. Spend time playing with her toys at the other end of the room, something few dogs can watch without joining in. Do some obedience work. Stop babying her. Leave her food down in the kitchen twice a day for a half hour only. No snacks. Three days later Pretty was "her old self."

### POINTS TO PONDER
- If you give a dog attention for something, she'll probably do it again.
- If you're upset, the dog will be more upset.

## Solutions to Common Dog/Baby Problems

### Barking or Nudging for Attention

Many dogs use a paw on the leg or a nudge of a nose to remind you to pet them. Do not give in to this form of canine blackmail. Tossing him a cookie, petting him, smiling at him, or otherwise rewarding him teaches him to do it more. Not only is this an intrusive behavior, but it is disrespectful. Dogs who do not respect people are the most likely to develop aggression and other problems. In canine terms, he is being the boss and you are following his orders. He could also inadvertently scratch or wake the baby.

Stopping this behavior is easy if you give the dog what he wants—just not the way he wants it. Leave a lead and collar on the dog when you are home, this way you can instantly put him through his paces. If the dog barks for attention, you say to yourself, "Fine, you want my attention, you have it!" and you do one minute of rigorous obedience. Use whatever commands he knows. If he only knows sit then it's sit, OK, sit, OK, sit, OK. Work him quickly, insist on immediate compliance, give him no praise, then drop the lead and ignore him. He may well choose to go do something else for a while. It's similar to a child coming up and saying, "I'm bored," and you responding "OK, well, the garage needs cleaning." Chances are the child will suddenly have a long list of things he'd rather be doing.

Lastly, be sure to praise him when he's leaving you alone like a good dog. It's just as important to notice the good as it is to correct the bad.

## Dog Licks Too Much

This sweet, though not necessarily wanted, behavior is a reflection of affection from the dog. We kiss, dogs lick. Again, and as always, have the lead and collar on your dog. If he licks the child more than you'd like, command "No lick" in a firm, nonangry tone, and then give a sideways snap on the lead. Immediately make him sit, guiding him into position if necessary. Once he complies, verbally praise him. If you attempt to touch him, chances are he'll lick you. It is important to always replace an unwanted behavior with a wanted one, in this case following "No lick" with "Sit. Good dog." This teaches him exactly what you would prefer him to do. Eventually, when he has the urge to lick, he'll sit instead.

## Dog Growls at the Baby

If you have done your homework, this is unlikely. You have already exposed her to children, so children are nothing new. Although most growling is due largely to confusion, all growling must be taken seriously. Seek professional assistance immediately, from either an experienced trainer or behaviorist. This is definitely not something you "wait and see" about. Aggression rarely heals itself. Its normal course, without intervention, is to steadily increase. The good news is most dogs that growl can be successfully trained not to. Just don't wait. Few people believe their beloved pet will bite, but every year many do. And most of those spent many months growling before ever trying to bite.

## Dog Mouths Baby

This is most often a friendly, if inappropriate, gesture on the dog's part. Retrievers classically have this problem, as they have been selected for generations to pick things up in their mouths. The highest compliment from a retriever is to retrieve a piece of you. They must, however, be taught not to do this.

First, correct him for doing this to you. The number of people who have learned to accept a canine mouth on them is amazing. If you allow the dog to do this to you, surely he will do it to children. Not only could mouthing frighten a child, but the child might be inadvertently scratched or pinched when he pulls away. When the dog mouths, tell him calmly but firmly "No bite." Move your body toward him, sound serious. Most dogs understand this as a threat and withdraw. Now, praise him verbally. If you try to pet him, he will probably mouth again, so don't. Instead, have him sit; then tell him how wonderful he is!

If this is not sufficient, start a good overall training program. Leave his lead and collar on him. When he mouths, pick up the lead, command "No bite," and give him a sideways correction (horizontal snap of the lead). That should make him stop for a moment, at which point you insert a desired behavior like "Sit," and then verbally praise him. Do not allow any mouthing of any kind. Those days are over.

## Dog Grabs Blanket

Chances are you have played Tug-of-War with your dog. Your dog enjoys this game, so when he feels like playing, he starts the game on his own by grabbing your clothing, a towel, or your baby's blanket. The more strongly you protest, the better your dog likes it, interpreting your attempts to yank the thing out of his mouth and your loud scoldings as all part of the game. You think he's being difficult. He thinks you are having fun. It's a classic dog/owner miscommunication.

First of all, the Tug-of-War must end. Instead, teach him the games discussed on pages 60 to 63. Teach him tricks (two of which are taught on pages 58 and 59). Engage that eager little mind of his. Secondly, teach him "Out," which means spit it out of your mouth. This is taught, as always, with lead and collar on. Holding the lead in one hand, give your dog something that he'll take but doesn't adore. Make sure it is too large to swallow or hide inside his mouth. Then, holding on to one side of it, tell him calmly and firmly, "Out." Chances are he won't, since he hasn't the foggiest idea what you mean. If this is true, give the lead a quick, abrupt, downward snap. Do not pull on the object. Pulling will only encourage him to hold on tighter! He must release it himself if he is to learn what the command means. Usually the dog opens his mouth, at which point you hold the object behind your back, and praise him warmly. Repeat. Soon he'll drop it like a hot potato. As he improves, use increasingly tempting things. The more difficult the object is for him to resist, the more enthusiastic your praise must be when he complies.

## Dog Jumps Up

Because the dog is on lead, you can easily manage him. Because you have spent lots of time lately training him to keep all four feet on the ground, he knows what to expect. Do the following: with the lead on, step on it at the point where it hits the ground when he is standing. This way, he will correct himself when he jumps up. When doing this, remain absolutely passive, ignore him, wait for him to come to his senses. After a few unsuccessful jumps, he'll stop. Now, tell him to sit, and then praise him warmly for controlling his wiggling, happy self. If, when you praise him, he tries again to jump, simply ignore him again until he settles back down. A few days of this, and he'll get the message.

## Dog Eats Diapers

When Sarah was an infant her parents gave away their Poodle, Coco, because she constantly tried to rip off Sarah's diapers. This sudden "viciousness" worried all concerned, as she was normally a lovely dog. Where did this frightening behavior come from? The answer lay in her mothering. Female dogs eat their puppies' waste for the first three weeks. Coco was just trying to keep Sarah clean, not attack her. Truth be told, most dogs enjoy feces of all kinds. They love rolling in it and eating it. Some are cat-box addicts, and others just indulge in the occasional horse pile, but most eat poop. Thus diapers can be a real temptation. Get a good diaper pail with a tight lid. Store bags of dirty diapers in a dogproof area. You'll never want a friendly lick again if you ever catch your dog indulging in a dirty diaper.

## Finding a Good Trainer

Locating a reputable trainer with the experience and talent to help you effectively is not too difficult. First, get referrals from local humane societies, shelters, and veterinarians. Don't take their word as gospel, but if a certain name comes up repeatedly, that's a good sign. Call the Better Business Bureau and Consumer Affairs to make sure the trainers are reputable.

Next, call the trainers. Chat with them about your dog and their methods. Ask them how long they have been training. What is their experience? Someone who trained dogs for the military may not be what you're looking for to help you with your nervous Shetland Sheepdog. What books and trainers do they like? Ask if they can give you references from people who've had the same types of problems you're having. Ask if you can come observe them work.

Always go with your gut instincts. This person will be in your home; if you don't like him over the phone, don't go further. There is no licensing in the field, anyone can call himself a trainer. Avoid people who hard-sell you. Anyone who hits, slaps, pins, hangs, or yells at the dog is no professional. You're paying for better ideas than that! Always keep in mind that you are hiring this person. Anywhere along the way, you can stop the proceedings, question what is going on, or fire him. That's the joy of being the one writing the check.

A good trainer trains you. Look for someone who spends as much time educating you as they do working with the dog. Then do your part and practice. Learning takes time for both you and your pet; practice is the only sure road to success.

## What If It Doesn't Work Out?

There are dogs who don't like babies. There aren't many of them, but they do exist. Some dogs become too frightened, a few are too aggressive, and others are just plain spoiled. It is no sin to decide that your dog would be better off in another home. What is a shame is when people pretend all is well and only take action after there is an incident. Most aggression is predictable, preventable, and correctable *if* appropriate action is taken as soon as there are signs of a problem.

Get professional help. Read up on dog training and behavior. Neuter the dog. Give it your best shot, but if in the end there is still a problem, find him a home. Don't feel guilty. Dogs come into this world with their own personalities. You can influence them, but you cannot change them. If yours isn't the right home, find one that is. Tell everyone you know that you're looking to place him. Put ads in the local paper. If your dog is a purebred, call the breeder first and see if she'll help. Most good breeders will help in any way they can. Contact the national club and ask if they have a rescue group. A pure-breed rescue group is a wonderful way to place your dog. Be honest about your dog. Continue his training, as that will make him easier to place. Make sure his shots are up to date.

When someone comes to look at the dog, get references and check them. Also take each person's name, address, and phone number, and tell them you'll call to let them know. These two simple acts help prevent unethical people from taking your pet and selling it for laboratory use. There are good homes out there; just screen carefully to make sure you've really found one.

## YOU NEVER KNOW

The McGuires purchased a German Shepherd pup who turned out to be very active. The McGuire household was a busy one, and the pup was constantly barking and getting in the way. They took her to training class and tried to be patient, but finally admitted that this pup was making them crazy. They started looking for a good home for her. Eventually a friend, Bill, came forward. He wanted a companion for his 20-month-old daughter, as well as a watchdog. They all agreed, and off the pup went.

A couple of weeks later, Bill called to report on his wondrous new dog. His little girl had wandered off. He heard wild barking. He ran toward the sound and found his new dog firmly planted between his child and the banks of a pond. The dog was doing her best to stop the little girl, blocking her path while barking in protest. Bill got to his daughter in time and is now convinced that he owns the smartest, best dog in the world—although he would prefer it if she barked more!

### POINTS TO PONDER
- Some dogs just irritate some people; it doesn't happen often, but it does happen.
- If you decide to find another home for your pet, tell everyone you know, and then be patient. Good homes are out there.

# 4

# *The Family Dog and the Toddler*

*"Out of sight is into trouble."*

The woman on the phone was distraught. "My son's dog snapped at my grandchild. That animal is not safe! Please will you help?"

I called the father. The story went like this: The father was standing in the kitchen, and through the window he saw his two-and-a-half-year-old son run up to his sleeping dog, giving it a well-placed kick. The dog yelped with pain, spun around, snapped at the child. The child, surprised, burst into tears.

I lambasted the father for leaving his toddler alone in the yard with the dog. No child that age is responsible enough to be left alone with an animal. That father is lucky he did not have to go to the hospital! The dog had the means and the motive to do serious harm; the fact that he didn't is a tribute to his fine temperament. That is one good dog.

Although some dogs tolerate just about anything from a human being, that should not be expected or required. Do not allow your child to do to a dog what you would not allow done to another child.

## S.A.F.E. First and Foremost

Dogs and toddlers should NEVER be left unsupervised. Even the kindest dog will react when cornered by a child trying to measure the depth of the canine ear with the sharp end of a pencil. It is the parents' job to keep the dog and child S.A.F.E.:

**S**upervise. Keep them in your vision at all times or physically separated—child in play pen or dog in crate. And we mean at all times. From the stories we hear, the majority of problems occur when adult eyes are elsewhere. It's astounding just how quickly a dog and a child can make mischief. Keep them in your sight!

**A**nticipate. A dog only has a few ways of protesting. He can move away, hop up on furniture, or go under a bed. Once the dog has done this, he has no other means to stop a child other than a bark, growl, or nip. If you see your dog retreating from a child, stop that child! Anticipate problems before they happen. Do not expect your dog to tolerate something you wouldn't.

**F**ollow through. If you say it, mean it. If you tell your child to stop bothering the dog, enforce that. If you tell the dog to sit, make him. All things are easier if your child and dog know that you mean what you say, and say what you mean.

**E**ducate. This means both the dog and the child. Teach your child by word and example that animals are to be treated with care. Do not allow hitting, teasing, or other harassment. Teach your dog by practice and patience that people—children in particular—make mistakes, and how to behave when those mistakes happen.

If you keep them both S.A.F.E., you have done your best to prevent the preventable.

## Moving Violations

Adults often play with a dog by kneeling down, making excited noises like "Hey, pup! What do I have?" while dragging a toy in front of him. The dog pounces on the toy. "Whee!" and the game begins.

Enter a toddler. She kneels down to play with some toy. She's making exciting noises while she moves the toy back and forth in front of her. The dog thinks "Playtime!" and pounces on her hand. Toddler screams. Dog, thinking the game has begun, gets more excited. Parents intervene: "Bad dog!" The dog is utterly confused.

Avoid this by starting play with a word instead of an action. Sit on the floor. Have the dog "Sit." Drag a toy slowly back and forth in front of him. Tell him calmly, "Wait." If he gets up, direct him to sit. When the dog is staying seated, excitedly tell him "OK, playtime!" and encourage him to play. Let him play for a minute or so; then tell him "Enough, sit." Immediately calm down. Repeat until he waits for the words "OK, playtime!" before pouncing. When he gets good at this, start moving more quickly or sounding more excited while he waits. Dogs love this game. Sitting there, trembling with excitement, awaiting the magic words.

Later, if you see your dog misinterpreting a child's game, a quick "Enough, sit" will give you immediate control, and the dog an immediate understanding that this is not the right time or place. Be sure to enthusiastically praise when he complies. If he does not respond to your verbal command, do not hesitate to put on his lead and practice with him. Set up the situation when you have complete control. He'll soon catch on, and when he does, heap on lots of praise!

## Table Manners

Like people, dogs must be taught basic table manners. A dog's uncontained enthusiasm for food—yours or his—can lead to trouble, particularly with children in the home.

### Dog Lunges at Food

First, is the dog hungry? If your dog is on a low-quality food, wormy, or just not being fed enough, there may be a very good reason he's acting like a wild man around your dinner. Feed him a good-quality food twice a day in the amount recommended. For pups under four months, ask your veterinarian or breeder how many meals to feed. Take a fecal sample to the vet to make sure your dog does not have worms. If all checks out well, then let's stop this unwanted behavior.

Before we can change his behavior, do we have to change yours? Is anyone feeding him from the table? If you want him to stop, you must stop. It's not fair to expect a dog to control himself if you can't control yourself. This includes everyone in the family!

### "Leave It"

"Leave it" is what you say when you want your dog to leave something alone, like your dinner, or the baby's pacifer. Teach this command with your dog on lead using a plain biscuit as bait. Holding his lead in one hand, show him the mild temptation in the other. Tell him "Leave it" in a calm, no-nonsense voice. If he reaches for it, give a quick sideways snap and then release.

When he stops pulling toward the food, immediately praise him. Then tell him "OK" and give him a small piece. This is an easy choice: control yourself and get the treat, or lunge and get a correction. Continue to work on lead, using increasingly attractive food until he resists anything you hold out. This is one of the easiest commands to teach. Just keep at it, he'll learn.

Here are two problems commonly encountered when teaching the "Leave it" command.

### Dog Grabs the Food before the OK

Try holding the food farther away from your dog. Also, make sure the leash is loose between corrections. If you hold him back, you're not allowing him to learn; you're doing his work for him. He is supposed to try for the food; that's the idea. When he does, you'll be ready. He'll learn that grabbing doesn't work. Allow your dog to learn! Let him make mistakes when you're ready for him. Correct him just as he tries to grab. Praise him and give a treat when he controls himself.

### Dog Takes the Food Roughly

Make sure he's on lead and you're ready to correct. Take a piece of food he's not too wild about, hold it in a closed fist (this protects your fingers), and offer it to him. If he grabs too hard, command "Easy," and give a snap on the lead. Repeat until he approaches with some hesitation. When he is gentle, allow him to take the food while you calmly praise him. Repeat with increasingly tempting delicacies. Most dogs catch on to this quickly.

## Food Bowl Safety

Ideally, dogs should be left alone when eating, but children do not always obey the rules. It is vital that you prepare the dog for possible food bowl invasions, teaching the dog to enjoy someone approaching his bowl. Always do this type of training out of sight of your children. We don't want them imitating you.

STEP 1. Start slowly. For the first few days, give your pet a small amount of his food at a time. When he finishes each portion, put a bit more in his bowl. Complete his whole meal this way, letting him clean his plate between each addition. Soon he will eagerly anticipate your arrival.

STEP 2. Once the dog happily awaits your coming to his bowl, start adding in the food while he is still eating. Do this over another few days, until he is completely relaxed about you coming over while he is eating.

STEP 3. When this is going well, put down the whole meal at once. As he eats, go over and add in an exciting treat like a bit of meat or cheese. Do this a few times a meal. Be sure to speak to him kindly as you approach. Keep this up for a day or two.

STEP 4. Now he is ready to have you start stroking him as you drop in the extras. Continue your friendly banter. After a few days of this, move on to the next stage.

STEP 5. Go to your dog as he eats, pick up the bowl midmeal, add in some yummies, and then put it immediately back down. Stay and stroke him for a moment. Most dogs don't mind this at all, once they realize you're adding in some extra treats.

STEP 6. Once he is totally relaxed about all of this, begin putting your hand in as he eats. Praise him with a happy voice.

### Going the Extra Mile

Still relaxed? Run toward the bowl, drop in a treat. Gently bump into him while he eats, drop in a treat. Roll toys near him and lunge to retrieve them—imitate a kid. Even if your child is well-mannered, your child's friends may not be, so prepare your dog for all eventualities by teaching him that people may be a bit annoying and bumbling but they mean well and bear good things. *If your dog glares at you, freezes midchew, or growls during any of this training, or if you feel nervous for any reason, get help from a competent local trainer or behaviorist.*

## GOOD INTENTIONS, BAD IDEA

Davis had not been a stable pup, yet he had coped surprisingly well with the addition of an infant. I had not heard from the Goldsteins for months when I received a call. "Davis is growling at the baby," Andrew said frantically. We set an appointment for that evening.

We sat in their living room, with their adorable little boy, Zach, crawling around the floor. As Zach turned toward the dog, Davis gave a low growl. "When did this start?" I asked, not feeling very hopeful. I had come on the Goldstein scene after they had worked with three trainers and been through two obedience classes. Davis found it just about impossible to calm himself, and it took calm commands and slow, firm techniques to get him in line. He was a longshot with kids in the first place, and this was not good.

"About a week ago," Andrew said. "We wanted Davis to get used to the baby, so we started holding Davis on the floor in our lap and letting the baby crawl on him while we praised him."

"That exercise did two things," I said. "It put Davis in a situation of being between you and the baby, which brought out his possessiveness, and secondly, you forced him to endure being mauled. What else could he do? He could not escape, so his only option was to growl."

I started them on a program of giving attention to Davis only when the baby approached him, the rest of the time the dog was ignored. If the baby got too close, they were to calmly divert the child. They also were to give Davis some time alone. Davis had been a nine-to-five dog, and I suspected that all this constant company, while pleasant, was stressing him. The Goldsteins set up a baby gate and put Davis' bed in the kitchen, making the dog a nice, safe retreat. I gave Davis one week to show vast improvement, or I was going to recommend placing him in another home. Happily he improved.

### POINTS TO PONDER

• Don't force your dog to interact with your baby. This puts him in a position of feeling trapped. Dogs who feel trapped can either run or fight. Davis could not flee, so he had no other option than to growl.

• Give your dog a safe haven. His crate, a gated room, someplace he can go that your child can't. We all need to take a break occasionally, and your dog is no exception.

• Reward the dog when the child is around; this will go a long way to improving your dog's opinion of his new family member.

• Get help quickly when you need it. The Goldsteins got help immediately and solved their problem quickly. If it had gone on much longer, they might not have been so successful in changing Davis' mind about their son.

# 5

# The Family Dog
# and Young Children

*"Don't buy a dog for your child.*
*Buy a dog for your family."*

This is Amy's dog. She wanted it. She's the one who's going to train it!" said Mrs. Towns from the counter, where she was making herself a cup of coffee. Seven-year-old Amy sat silently at the table. Mom was peeved. "I work all day. I don't need another thing to take care of. Amy forgets to feed the dog. She doesn't walk it. I end up doing it all. That wasn't the deal."

I tried to break the news to her gently. "You're right that dogs are a lot of work, and you're right that Amy needs to pitch in, but a pet is a family project. Why don't we all sit down and decide what needs to be done and who can do it." Amy looked relieved.

Children cannot care for pets without help. Caring for a dog can be challenging for adults; it is close to impossible for a child. Many parents acquire the pet in the hopes of instilling responsibility in their child. Caring for a pet can do this, with the help of the parents.

## Making Your Dog Everyone's Responsibility

Over the years, we've found some easy ways to make dog ownership the family project that we all want it to be. This chapter contains many of these ideas.

### Write Down the Dog Related Chores

List all the chores—from shopping for pet food to scooping the yard, from trips to the vet to picking up toys. This is to make sure that you adults get the credit you deserve for some of the weekly and monthly tasks the kids don't ever really think about. Now make a list of daily chores. It might look like this: feed Princess, water Princess, train Princess, pick up dog toys, clean up dog yard, walk Princess, play with Princess, brush Princess.

Now imagine this is a four-member household that includes Mom, Dad, Jack, and Marie. Jack is seven and Marie is five. We recommend clearly dividing up the chores by days of the week. Some people choose Monday, Wednesday, etc. Others assign one child odd days and the other evens. If there is any confusion about this, simply marking a large calendar with a magic marker, one color for each child, or with different stickers, solves any problems. Even a small child can learn to recognize his color or sticker. Now that you have the days straightened out, make a chart of chores that need doing, gather the family together, and decide who does what with whom.

Here's a sample:

| | Mom | Dad | Jack | Marie |
|---|---|---|---|---|
| Feed Princess | Even | Odd | Odd | Even |
| Water Princess | | | Odd | Even |
| Train Princess | Odd | Even | Even | Odd |
| Pick up dog toys | | | Odd | Even |
| Pick up dog yard | Even | Odd | | |
| Walk Princess | Odd | Even | | |
| Play with Princess | Even | Odd | Even | Odd |
| Brush Princess | Even | Odd | | |

Such a schedule can be reviewed and revised monthly or weekly, whenever the need arises. Please note: the adults have more responsibility than the kids. As the kids mature, they can take on more of the burden. But until then, you'll be doing most of it.

## Walking the Dog

Most children should NOT walk the dog unattended. Dogs, even small ones, are incredibly strong, and unless the animal is extremely well-behaved, a child walking a dog unattended is a dangerous situation. As a general guideline, if the dog is heavier than one fifth of your child's weight, it's too big for him or her to walk.

## Exercising the Dog

Note that this is split into parent/child teams. Both of these children are too young to exercise the dog by themselves. Playing with the dog in teams gives everyone some nice time together. Alternatively, you can drink your tea, read the paper, or just enjoy the day, but you need to have an eye on them both.

## Feeding the Dog

Even small children can assist with getting the bowl, washing it out, filling it, giving it to the dog. This last one ONLY if your dog is nonaggressive and controlled around food. The adult job is to supervise amounts and make sure the dog is under control. A good canine habit to develop is making the dog sit until the food bowl is put down. Then have the child release him with a happy "OK, good dog!"

## Watering the Dog

Reminding an adult to fill the water bowl, washing out the bowl daily, and wiping up the spills are all appropriate tasks for the youngest dog owner. Older children can do the feeding and watering themselves.

### Picking Up Toys

It is always a good idea to rotate dog toys, leaving three or four down at a time and putting the rest away. This way the dog will stay more interested in them. Most children can assist with this.

### Cleaning Up the Yard

Yuck. Rotate this one among all able-bodied family members. It is too easy to dump the cleanup chore on the kids; don't do it. Sharing this job among everyone teaches the child more about fairness and responsibility than any discussion.

### Grooming the Dog

Whether or not a child can assist you with this is largely determined by what kind of coat your dog has and how tolerant he or she is of brushing. Some dogs love it. These dogs can be groomed by children under the supervision of an adult.

### Making It Work

We all need to be told we've done a good job. Most of us are more willing to remind about a chore not remembered than to say something nice about a task well done. Even if you have to remind a youngster to fill the water bowl, be sure to let her know that she did a good job.

## Training the Dog

*Please note: If you do not have control over the dog, do not start these exercises. First teach your dog to listen and respond consistently to you. There are numerous excellent training manuals, videos, classes, and private instructors available; our favorite books and video are listed in the bibliography. Once your dog listens to you, then start including your child. Never ask the child to do something with the dog that you cannot.*

Training is the best way to teach a dog to respect a child. Once a dog will follow a child's command, it will be less likely to steal a toy from, jump up on, knock over, run into, or otherwise be rude to the child. But— and here's a big but—this requires adult supervision at all times, much like using a knife. If a child attempts this himself and fails, the dog learns that the child is incapable of asserting control. This is the last thing you want the dog to know. You want the dog to believe that the child is fully able to manage him. This will give the child psychological control long before he can manage physical control.

Start with the dog on lead. The child's job is to give a clear command in a confident voice while standing up straight. The adult's job is to silently but firmly enforce the command if the dog does not respond to the child. Say nothing and make no eye contact with the dog. The less the dog associates the enforcement with you, the adult, the better. The focus here needs to be the dog/child interaction.

Once the dog obeys, the child praises the dog. When the dog responds consistently to the child's command, then practice the same command in more-distracting situations. Have the child command "Sit," and then open the front door. Have the child command "Sit" while holding the dog's food bowl. Again, you handle the dog's lead and allow the child to attempt only those commands that you and the dog can accomplish easily on your own.

When the dog is responding to these more-difficult situations, then have the child begin to hold the leash, with the adult placing the dog in position when necessary. When the child starts to take control, work in a quiet place with few distractions. This will make it easier for both the dog and your child to concentrate.

Even though your child is growing up, it is still important to keep things S.A.F.E. (Supervise, Anticipate, Follow through, Enforce). It is all too easy to let everyone out into the backyard to play, but unless you can keep half an eye on things easily, don't do it. Anticipate problems. If your dog is frightened by loud noises, crate him in a quiet place while your child plays with a rowdy toy. Does your dog chase moving things? Keep him inside while everyone bikes in the driveway. Follow through with commands and instructions more than ever. When you tell the dog "Sit," make sure he does. When you tell your child "Stop it," make sure she does. This is not the time to get lax with your expectations and start repeating yourself. If you do, both dog and child will soon learn they can easily ignore you.

## *Tricks*

One fun thing to do that is good for both the child and the dog is teaching the dog tricks. Not only does this develop the child's control over the dog, and the dog's respect for the child, but it's fun for everyone. When training is fun, everyone tends to do it more often.

### Shake

Here's a classic: the child says "Shake," and the dog holds out his paw obligingly. Millions of dogs have learned this amusing trick, and millions of kids have delighted in teaching it. Raising a paw is a submissive gesture, so it is a good mental exercise for the dog.

Start with the dog sitting. Command "Shake," and gently grasp the paw and shake it. Immediately release the paw. Give lots of praise! Tell him how high his IQ is, how quick, willing, or handsome he is! Repeat four or five times each session. Usually in a week or so, the dog will respond to the command with a raised paw and a wagging tail. Fun for everyone!

Do not allow the child to hold on to the dog's paw or to squeeze it. Dogs don't like either. Any discomfort or restraint will slow down the learning process and cause some dogs to mouth the child in protest.

## Bang

The child says "Bang," and points at the dog. The dog rolls over, sticking his feet in the air. If you own a dog who enjoys having his belly rubbed, "Bang" is an easy command to teach. Not only is this cute, but it is another submissive posture for the dog. Showing submission on your child's command is excellent for the dog and a good behavioral barometer. If one day your dog refuses to roll on his back on command, you probably have some trouble brewing. Have the dog evaluated by a professional and sign up for a local obedience class immediately.

Begin this training with your dog lying on something soft like a rug or carpet. Walk over to him. Command "Bang" with a "pistol finger" hand signal. Reach down, gently roll him on his back, and scratch his belly. Tell him what a marvelous dog he is. Brilliant! Beautiful! The best! Then stand up and ignore him. Usually the dog will lie there on his back expectantly for a few moments before flopping back to his side. Immediately say "Bang" again, and repeat as above. Soon he'll flip delightedly onto his back, anticipating a belly rub the moment he hears "Bang!"

## Good Games, Bad Games

Nancy, a young mother, stared at her pup, Maxie, in frustration. "Max's making me crazy. I can't walk two steps in my robe without him attacking me. He grabs toys away from David all the time. He bites hard. Do you think we have to get rid of him?" She sounded worried.

"Maxie looks like the type of pup who would love Tug-of-War," I said, glancing at the big Rottweiler puppy sleeping under the coffee table.

"Oh, yes, he loves it! Max'll play that forever," Nancy said with a smile.

"Well, that's a big part of your problem," I said, then went on to explain the problems she had inadvertently caused with this popular but bad game. Tug-of-War teaches the pup that you like it when he fights with you. Never train a puppy or adult dog to do anything with you that you don't want him to do with your child.

Bad games foster combat and competition between human and canine. Any game that involves play fighting with the dog (wrestling), competing for possession of an object (Tug-of-War), or one that has you following the dog's lead (Chase!) are to be avoided.

Good games promote cooperation and control. Games like Fetch, Beat the Clock, Hide and Seek, and all manner of tricks are great. Good games develop the working relationship between you and your pet as well as reinforcing your leadership. Having a good dog is largely a matter of teaching the dog self-control. A good dog—and a safe dog around children—sits when he wants to jump, resists when he wants to take, and releases what he wants to hold on to. Anything you can do to foster that kind of control is all for the good. Everything you do with your dog teaches him something! Make sure you're teaching him the right things!

## Fetch

In Fetch you throw something that your dog brings back. Some dogs adore this game. Some dogs could care less. If your dog doesn't like it, then skip it. Many dogs refuse to return the toy, dashing out of reach at the last possible instant and turning Fetch into a less productive game of Chase! This can be avoided if you reward the dog for bringing the toy to you rather than trying to grab it out of his mouth. Start playing in a confined area. Toss the toy, and when the dog gets it, squat down and encourage him to return to you. When he does, do NOT grab the toy. Instead, pet him and tell him how smart he is to come back. After ten or more seconds, quietly take the toy and throw it. Soon he'll realize that returning to you is fun!

If he is a die-hard dasher, then put a long line on him—fifteen feet or so of rope. When he dashes away, reel him in calmly, pet him for being such a good dog, then calmly take the toy. Follow this with more praise and play.

Another alternative is simply bring along more than one toy. Throw one and when he retrieves it, get his attention and toss the other. Most dogs will drop the one they have to pursue this new item and around you'll go. Terrific exercise for the dog with minimal effort on your part.

## Hide and Seek

Great fun for everyone! Start with one person holding the dog while another hides. Once the person—in this case, Johnny—is hidden, you say "Where's Johnny? Find Johnny," and you walk with the dog through the house. At first, Johnny may have to make some noise to attract the dog's attention. Once the dog finds him, everyone should praise him and tell him how bright he is. Soon the dog will charge around with no encouragement, finding each family member by name. Not only is this a great rainy-day energy burner, but it just might come in handy one day.

## Find It

This is Hide and Seek with objects. Beloved toys or biscuits are easiest to start with. Have a friend hold the dog while you place the toy or biscuit a few feet away in plain sight. Return to the dog and say "Where's the biscuit? Find it. Find the biscuit," and let him go. If he bolts to the biscuit, great. If not, walk him back to it and point it out; then praise him like he's a rocket scientist when he finds it. As he gets better, make the hiding places harder and harder. Dogs can learn many toys and objects by name playing this game. This is a wonderful rainy-day game for the kids to play with their canine friend.

## Beat the Clock

This high-speed game teaches your dog to respond instantly to commands when excited or distracted, something every dog needs help with. Put your dog on lead and start to romp with him. Tell him "OK, playtime!" Speak excitedly, jump around—anything to get him happy and interested. Right in the middle of the festivities, give him a command. Immediately become still and silent. Guide him into position if need be. The moment that he obeys, instantly restart the game. If you do this correctly, being very happy and exuberant during the play and absolutely silent and still after commands, your dog will quickly learn how to "turn on" the game by obeying you immediately.

# 6

# Dogproofing Your Child

*"Always take a dog seriously."*

This chapter is for adults who want the children in their lives to be safe around dogs. It's for all children: the ones that love dogs and the ones that don't, the ones that are frightened of the friendly mutt down the street and the ones that want to pet every dog they see. No matter who your child is or what they think about dogs, there are some simple rules that everyone should follow when interacting with any dog. Along with those few rules, an understanding of basic canine body language will make it easier to judge which canines are friendly and which ones aren't.

Dogs are great. They love us, protect us, play with us, and are our friends. But just like people, not every dog is friendly and not every dog likes kids. Luckily dogs can "talk" to us, if we know how to "listen." Dogs talk with their bodies. When we understand their body language, we'll have a better understanding of dogs.

This chapter teaches adults how to educate their children about understanding what a dog is "saying" and what rules to follow, so that every interaction the children have with a dog will be a safe one.

## A Telling Tail

To begin this section, read the following story yourself, then read through the follow-up. After that, read the story to your child and talk about the follow-up together. Allow the child to guess, and support all attempts to figure it out independently. An idea a child comes to in his own mind is usually much better remembered than something he is told. Make sure you both touch on all the points before you move on.

*Two girls are walking down the street, they're about nine years old. Walking toward them is a woman with her dog. One girl, seeing the dog, says to her friend, "What a cute dog!" and runs toward it. The owner steps between the dog and the girl saying "My dog doesn't like—" But the girl doesn't listen. "Oh, he's so adorable!" she says, reaching toward the dog. The dog backs away, head down, tail tucked, eyes wide. "Really, this is not a good—" The dog is now backed to the end of his lead. The girl reaches out to pet the dog, and he growls.*

## What did the girl do wrong?

**She ran at the dog.** Probably like you, the dog did not like a stranger running at him. It is always best to move slowly around a dog and to let him come to you when saying hello.

**She did not listen to the owner.** Always ask the owner if you can pet the dog. Respect whatever answer she gives. She knows the dog better than anyone. If the owner says don't touch—even if you think the dog looks friendly—take her word for it. If the owner is not around, leave the dog alone!

**She did not introduce herself to the dog.** You wouldn't run up to a stranger on the street and try to touch him. That would be rude and strange. It is not so different for a dog. Always stand still and speak to a dog calmly. If he's feeling friendly, he will come up to you.

**She did not pay attention to what the dog was doing**. If you really love dogs, then don't frighten them. Dogs can't tell you in words "Hey, I'm scared of you!" They can only show you how they feel. Dogs show you they are frightened by not coming up to you when you speak to them. This dog backed away, lowered his head, and tucked his tail between his legs, telling the girl in every way possible "Leave me alone!"

**She chased the dog.** When a dog backs away, he isn't kidding. He's telling you he doesn't feel friendly at that moment. No matter how well you know the dog, or how friendly you think he is, if a dog backs away from you, leave him alone.

## Body Language

Dogs don't talk, but they do communicate. Understanding what a dog is saying to you is the best way to stay safe. Here's the quick and easy guide to canine body language:

### Aggressive

If the dog is trying to appear larger by holding his tail and ears up and raising the hair on his back, then he is feeling aggressive. A dog in this posture may wag his tail. In this case, the quick, stiff, vertical wagging is excitement, not friendliness. Stay away from this dog.

### Fearful

If the dog is trying to appear smaller, crouching low to the ground with his head down, ears down, tail down or between his legs, mouth closed, he is frightened.

If this dog is approached, he may become aggressive out of fear. Leave this dog alone.

## Friendly

A relaxed dog stands up; his head is not way up or down; his ears may be forward or back; his mouth is relaxed and open; his tail is usually wagging. The tail is being carried somewhere below the line of the back but not between his hind legs. A relaxed dog is the dog to make friends with.

## Rules for Interacting with Dogs

**The owner must be present.** Even if you know the dog well, teach your child that the owner must be present and give the OK before the child may pet the dog. A dog who is friendly with the owner nearby may not be when alone.

**Let the dog come to you.** Teach your child to allow the dog to approach. A dog that voluntarily approaches a child is many times safer than a dog that is approached. When a dog comes toward you or your child in a friendly manner, it is basically saying "Yes, I would like to spend some time with you." Dogs that hang back or show no interest may be saying just the opposite.

**Move slowly.** Ask your child this simple question: "What do dogs like to chase?" There are many right answers—from balls to squirrels, from planes in the sky to bicycles on the sidewalk. After your child has come up with a few, ask her this: "Does a dog like to chase a tree?" Most kids will say "No" loud and clear. When asked why, kids usually know it's because the tree doesn't move. Right!

Lastly, ask "What will a dog do if you run away from it?" And most kids immediately make the mental leap and say "Chase me!" And that is the point. Dogs chase things that move. If your child is moving, the dog will chase her, whether she's on a bike, a skateboard, rollerblades, or just running. The faster your child is moving, the more likely the dog is to pursue. Doggy physics. If your child wants to be ignored by a dog, she should move slowly and calmly away from the animal.

**Speak calmly.** Most kids arrive on the planet with the volume knob turned up full. This can spook some dogs. Luckily, few dogs have been hurt or frightened by humans who were speaking calmly. For many dogs, a calm, warm tone of voice instantly relaxes them, the way a loving hug might relax a child. Teach your child to speak calmly around dogs.

**Don't stare.** In dog language, staring is a threat. When you say hello to a dog, look at his ears or his friendly wagging tail. Most friendly dogs don't mind some eye contact, but introduce yourself first. If you are ever confronted by a dog that is aggressive, look away! If you stare, you'll be asking for a fight!

### DON'TS

- Don't pet a dog if the owner is not around.
- Don't pet any dog on a chain, behind a fence, in a car.
- Don't grab at, hit, or chase a dog.
- Don't move quickly near a dog.
- Don't scream or yell near a dog.
- Don't stare at a dog.
- Don't pet a dog who is backing away or looks frightened.
- Don't pet a growling or barking dog.
- Don't hug a dog or try to kiss his face.
- Don't bend over or step over a dog.

# 7

# *Warning Signs*

*"Aggression is serious—once you've got it,
you must take action immediately."*

He's never done that before," Steve said, petting the Cocker's silky head. "He just lunged at me when I went to kiss my son good night. Totally out of the blue."

"Has he ever growled at anyone before?" I asked.

"He used to growl whenever he had a bone. Now, we leave him alone when he has something." Steve stopped petting the dog. The Cocker nudged Steve with his nose.

"Don't pet him," I instructed. The Cocker nudged again. Getting no response, he put both paws on the man's lap and barked softly.

"What is he doing?" asked the wife.

"He's giving your husband a command. This dog is very pushy. We have some work to do."

Dogs usually have to build up to a bite. They start with simple disobedience. They move on to challenges, threat gestures, growls, and then a bite. The first bite may surprise a novice owner, but to the experienced eye, it's as predictable as a storm rolling in. Our job in this chapter is to teach you to recognize that storm while it is still a long way away.

# Q and A

### *If I ignore it, won't it go away?*

No. Aggression either increases or decreases depending on what action you take. The truth is that canine aggression usually works. The dog snarls, you withdraw. He growls and you leave him alone. This confirms his belief that he can assert himself with you, making him more likely to be aggressive in the future.

### *People are telling me to get rough with my dog. Is that a good idea?*

No. Getting rough can vary from hanging the dog by the collar to hitting, from shaking by the neck to pinning the dog down. These techniques are often both ineffectual and dangerous! They can heighten the dog's defense response, increasing the frequency and intensity of his aggression.

It is true that your pet needs to be controlled but that is best done through training, not through abuse. A dog who is showing signs of aggression may well decide to discipline you for "attacking" him with a nip or worse. If you do succeed in manhandling or intimidating him into a semblance of submission, it is doubtful that your spouse or child will be able to repeat the performance!

Instead, seek professional assistance, train your dog to respond to commands, make him work for the things he wants, and limit the attention you give him: teach him in all ways that you are his leader and he is the beloved, cherished, and obedient follower. Aggression is most often a reflection of his general attitude toward you; change that, and many times the aggression will decrease.

## Signs That Aggression Is on Its Way

The first thing to know about aggression is that when caught early, it is usually correctable. The second thing to know is that healthy dogs don't "turn" on their owners without warning. There are clear signs that trouble is brewing. Not every dog who is aggressive will have all of these signs. Some will only have a couple. Most will have at least a few. If your dog has any of these signs, seek professional advice, join a training class, and train your dog.

### Ignores Known Commands

This is so common that most households figure this is just the way dogs are. Not so. Not only is ignoring commands a bad habit, but it can be a strong sign that your dog literally does not think you're worth listening to. And if he won't pay attention to you, an adult, what chance do your children have?

You taught him to ignore you by repeating commands. Aggression most often comes from a dog that sees himself as the head of the household. As long as everything goes his way, he's fine. Cross him, and you'll get growled at or worse. If your dog ignores you or walks away when you issue a command, take it seriously. Get the whole family involved! Set up rules that everyone will follow regarding jumping on furniture, eating from the table, and responding to commands. Make him obey a command before you do anything for him. Make sure everyone stops all the free attention he's been getting, or you could be headed for trouble. A united family front is an effective vehicle for change.

### Refuses to Lie Down on Command

Here's an even stronger indicator of a potential aggression problem. Lying down is the most submissive posture your dog can assume. If he refuses to learn this command, or if he has "forgotten it" of late, trouble is brewing. Get help. Withdraw all attention unless he is down. If the dog tenses up or growls, stop. Do not continue without a trainer's or behaviorist's help.

### Mounts You or the Children

As embarrassing as this is, your dog is not doing it because he thinks you are attractive. He is doing this as an act of dominance. And because it is about power and not about sex, a female dog can be a mounter as well, although that is less common. This neither funny nor acceptable behavior is always a sign that the dog thinks he is in charge. Trouble is most definitely on its way.

### Bumps into You or Children

Disrespectful dogs will bump into people they feel are below them in the group. If your child is being pushed out of the way at the door, bumped in the hall, and knocked down in the living room, this is no mistake! Keep the dog on lead and correct him when he crashes into your child. Make him sit while your child goes through the doorway ahead of him. Have your child work him on his commands if possible as outlined on pages 56 and 57. The more the dog obeys your child, the more he'll respect your child.

## Refuses to Give Up Sleeping Areas

Your dog is asleep on the couch. You tell him to get off, and he lowers his head, tensing. You feel threatened. A dominant dog doesn't relinquish sleeping areas to subordinates. And once a dog is elevated on a bed or couch, the likelihood of an aggressive incident increases. It also puts the dog at your child's face level—not good. A dog who shows any hint of aggression should stay on the floor.

## Stops Eating or Chewing When Approached

Your dog is chewing a toy. You walk toward him, and he stops. He looks at you tensely. If you make a move toward the toy, he either tenses up, growls, or moves his head between your hand and the toy, blocking you. This is not good. Nothing in your house is his. Toys, beds, bowls are all yours. You allow him to use them. He has absolutely no right to claim them as his own or warn you from them. If he's willing to compete with you, what will he be like with your children and their friends?

## Hides under Furniture

A dog who heads for cover is a dog who's saying "I'm frightened." Push too hard and you'll get a bite. Never allow a child to crawl under a piece of furniture toward the hiding dog! On the dog's behalf, this is usually an animal who has been harshly corrected and has lost trust in humans. Move to positive training methods. Leave a lead on the dog when you are home with him.

Stop all threatening and violent training methods. If he scoots under, call him happily and use the lead to guide him out; then praise him and give him a treat. Chances are he'll learn to relax. This will start rebuilding his faith in you. Prevent the problem by blocking the area with suitcases or boxes.

### Growls for Any Reason Other than Play

Growls are warnings. In play, they warn in fun. The same way kids shout "I'm gonna get you!" dogs growl in play. You can tell this is play because the tail is wagging, and the dog is moving in a playful, relaxed manner. There are also unsure growls, such as the low growl a dog gives an object that he does not recognize. This is not an aggressive growl as much as a commentary. Normally when the object has been thoroughly examined, the growling disappears.

Then there are the other growls, the "Don't come closer," "Don't bother me," "I don't want to do that" growls. These are bad news. The number of owners who tell us "He's just talking," "He's never liked having his feet handled," or some other excuse is astounding. Growls seldom stay at that level. Unchecked, they will sooner or later add up to a snap or worse. Get help.

## NINE WAYS TO PREVENT AGGRESSION

1. Neuter your dog at six months old.

2. Socialize and train your dog as young as possible.

3. Get him around nice children as early as you can.

4. Supervise children and dogs always.

5. Don't hit or yell at your dog.

6. Praise him warmly when he is behaving himself.

7. Don't play aggressively or roughly with him.

8. Make him respond to a command before you do anything for him.

9. Make him a member of the family. Tied to a tree is no place to be!

## *How to Get Professional Help*

The first person you should speak to is your veterinarian. Some aggression is related to health conditions. Once your vet gives him a clean bill of health, hire a reputable trainer. A good trainer uses...

### *... a variety of methods*

You want someone who'll be creative, matching the methods he or she selects to your needs and your dog's temperament. Ask the trainer what kind of equipment he uses. The answer should boil down to "Well, that depends on the dog."

### *... the least amount of force necessary to get the desired response*

Just about any dog can be dominated with brute force, but that does not make for a well-trained dog. Ask the trainer "What is the most extreme correction you use?" Hanging the dog by the collar, slapping, or hitting are hardly "training methods." What approaches will be used? The leash and collar are the tools, but it is an understanding of canine psychology and proper instruction that will give you the control you need. A successful training program teaches you as well as the dog.

### *... a great deal of praise*

Training should be fun for all concerned. Your dog's wagging tail and happy grin are testimony to how joyfully he obeys you. A good trainer has lots of ways of rewarding your dog and may use his or her voice, petting, treats, toys, or a good romp to reinforce good behavior. Look for results; good trainers get them quickly and with the dog's full cooperation.

# NEUTERING

Females, as they come into season, can easily live up to their title *bitch*. Males, chronically "in season," may be difficult to live with year-round. Neutering improves both sexes as pets. So why do owners resist this procedure? Here are some of the common things we hear:

**Neutering will make my dog fat and lazy.**
Actually, eating too much and not enough exercise makes dogs fat and lazy.

**Neutering will make my dog a wimp.**
Neutering is not brain surgery. Neutered pets remain protective of their homes.

**Shouldn't my dog have one litter?**
No! It does nothing for females and makes males harder to live with! Our society routinely kills millions of animals each year because there aren't enough homes! Do not add to the problem!

**I just can't think about it.**
You are not alone. Some women and most men have a gut (or lower) reaction to the idea of neutering. Please remember we are not talking about you!

The facts are that your dog will live a happier, healthier, and calmer life once neutered. His primary job is to be a good pet, and neutering will help him be just that. Every pet should be neutered.

## When All Else Fails

A few dogs are born dangerous. Another handful become dangerous as they mature. Such animals are not pets. How do you know if you have such a dog? He has tried to bite, or has bitten, people numerous times. Or a reliable expert has told you he will. You have sought out experts, and they tell you the animal is untrainable, or you have taken their advice and it has not helped. Give the animal every possible chance. Speak to several trainers or behaviorists; discuss it with your veterinarian. But if it comes down to the safety of your child, there is no choice, the dog goes.

If your dog's aggression is specifically focused on children, you may attempt to give the dog away. Don't be tempted to lie. That's easy, but it's not right. A child's welfare may well be at stake. Keep in mind that you could be held legally liable if a problem develops.

If your dog's aggression is directed at one and all, children and adults, your choice is even harder. The temptation is to give him away without explanation. By doing this you may feel like you "gave him a chance," but what you probably have done is caused fear and suffering for all concerned. Such dogs often get bounced from home to home, confused and unhappy. The truth is, you and your family are probably the best home that the dog can hope to find.

The right choice, if you have an intractable biter, is euthanasia. It is a terrible thing to have to do, but it can be the kindest way of dealing with a mentally unstable dog. The fact is the dog is not safe and cannot be made safe. In such situations, ending his life with kindness can be the last loving thing you do for this dog.

# Conclusion

Dogs somehow mesh with our families and lives like no other animal. They are our constant companions through their entire lives, blending in regardless of our age or need. They are unimpressed by riches or poverty, beauty or lack of it. Instead, they see our souls, who we really are, and love us for that and that alone.

Most dogs are incredibly good beings, taking all our strange behaviors in stride. The problems between our two species are largely due to miscommunication, not to any innate imperfection. Please remember always that dogs are traveling in our world without a map or dictionary. We are their guides, and it is up to us to teach them our customs, to learn theirs, and to show them the way while keeping them out of trouble. In exchange, they love us, play with us, protect us, and humor us until their last dying breath. As a salute to that, we leave you with one more true story.

Sarah's father used to commute by train, and every night, Sarah and her mother would walk the four long blocks to the train station to meet him. One evening her father got a ride home, but Sarah, a little over three years old at the time, did not know that. When the time came around, off she went, by herself, to meet him. Hannibal, their mixed-breed, tagged along. When Sarah's father arrived home a few minutes later, everyone noticed the two were missing.

As her family frantically searched the house, a knock came at the door. "Mr. Wilson?" the man said. "Don't you have a little girl?" Sarah's parents nodded, worried. "Well, she's down at the train station, sitting on the stone wall, and that dog of yours won't let anyone near her."

They rushed to the station and that was exactly true. Sarah sat, swinging her legs, happy as a lark waiting for her dad. Hannibal sat next to her, silently baring his teeth at anyone foolish enough to attempt touching her. To this day no one knows who was happier to see the other—Sarah's parents to find her or Hannibal to see them.

Hannibal was a beloved family dog, tolerant of the children and good with their friends. He had never shown aggression previously, but then "his" little girl had never wandered off before. He was just a good dog, like the one in your house right now. Fine animals, trying their best, making us happy.

We can never repay the dogs in our past for the gifts they have given us. We only hope that through this book, we enable you and your children to have the same kind of wonderful experiences with your animals that we have had with ours.

# *Bibliography*

**Good Owners, Great Dogs** (The Book)
*Brian Kilcommons with Sarah Wilson, Warner Books, 1992*

Not surprisingly, we love this text. We took care to make it fun
and easy to read, and we included over three hundred photos of
more than thirty breeds to create what we, and many others,
think is the most comprehensive dog training book for the pet-
owning public. Included are detailed sections on puppy training,
adult dog training, and problem correction. All of it is taught
in simple steps and highlighted with amusing stories and valu-
able tips.

    Available at most book stores and through 1-800-457-PETS.

**Good Owners, Great Dogs** (The Video)
*Brian Kilcommons and Sarah Wilson, Family Dog
Distribution, 1990*

The first tape ever recommended by the ASPCA. Divided into
short, easy-to-learn-from sections, this 57-minute VHS cassette
can be used as a stand-alone or as an excellent companion to the
book. Most of the dogs used in the tape were straight out of a
shelter, ensuring you that these methods work even on un-
trained, unruly dogs. Training puppies and adult dogs is clearly
demonstrated, and common problems such as pulling, jumping,
stealing food, housebreaking, chewing, mouthing, and rushing
out doorways are addressed.

    Available through 1-800-457-PETS.

### The Harper's Illustrated Handbook of Dogs
*Edited by Roger Caras, health section by Robert Kirk, DVM, and training section by Brian Kilcommons, Harper and Row Publishers, reprint 1990*

If you are looking for a dog, or want to learn more about the one you have, this well-illustrated, sensible book is a wonderful resource. It also has easy-to-use sections on health care, grooming, and general care, with a strong training piece by Brian. One of the best general books around and a useful addition to any dog owner's library.

### Don't Shoot the Dog!
*Karen Pryor, Bantam Books, 1985*

This wonderful text does not limit itself to dogs. Within its covers, you will find useful information on teaching everything and everyone from chimps to dolphins, from dogs to spouses. The author's style is witty and easy. The methods are humane, effective, and universally useful. We highly recommend it.

### Playtraining Your Dog
*Patricia Gail Burnham, St. Martin's Press, 1980*

Because this is a competitive obedience text, there are sections that the average pet owner will not understand or want to understand. There is, however, much wisdom in it, and the first two sections will help any dog owner understand and train his or her companion with more love, patience, and fun.

# Index